We are all dancers. We use movement to express ourselves—our hungers, pains, angers, joys, confusions, fears—long before we use words, and we understand the meanings of movements long before we understand those of words.

—FRANKLIN STEVENS

The Dance
NOTEBOOK

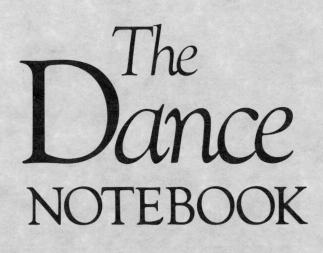

Movement never lies. It is a barometer telling the state of the soul's weather to all who can read it.

—MARTHA GRAHAM

Two dancers on the stage are enough material for me;
they are already a story in themselves.

—GEORGE BALANCHINE

*Dancing is not taught as an art in any university.
There, it is still in the gymnasium.*

—AGNES DE MILLE

*Let us consider as dance all rhythmical motion
not related to the work motif.*

—CURT SACHS

Dancing as an art, we may be sure, cannot die out, but will always be undergoing a rebirth. Not merely as an art, but also as a social custom, it perpetually emerges afresh from the soul of the people.

—HAVELOCK ELLIS

We look at the dance to impart the sensation of living in an affirmation of life, to energize the spectator into keener awareness of the vigor, the mystery, the humor, the variety, and the wonder of life.

—MARTHA GRAHAM

For the Indian, dance is a personal form of prayer. When the Eagle Dancer puts on his costume, when he begins to dance to the music, he doesn't simply perform it; he actually becomes the eagle itself. The dancer is virtually inseparable from the dance.

—JAMAKE HIGHWATER

The place of the dance is within the heart.

—TOM ROBBINS

I want to dance always, to be good and not evil, and when it is all over, not to have the feeling that I might have done better.

—RUTH ST. DENIS

It was hard for her. It was all so new. All those other girls, so thin, so strong, so good, so pretty, knew more steps than she did.

—TONI BENTLEY

All the disasters of mankind, all the misfortunes that histories are so full of, the blunders of politicians, the miscarriages of great commanders—all this comes from want of skill in dancing.

—JEAN BAPTISTE POQUELIN (MOLIÈRE)

The truest expression of a people is in its dances
and its music. Bodies never lie.

—AGNES DE MILLE

Dancing: wonderful training for girls. It's the first way you learn to guess what a man is doing before he does it.

—CHRISTOPHER MORLEY

There is no such thing as a wrong body for dance. The wrong body is a sick body, and that can be corrected spiritually.

—MARIE BROOKS

Dancing may not be the perfect substitute for love, human love, but it certainly requires all the time and thought and energy that could otherwise be dedicated to love.

—TONI BENTLEY

There's only one of me. There's only one of anybody. That's why steps look different on different people.

—JUDITH JAMISON

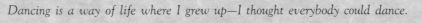

Dancing is a way of life where I grew up—I thought everybody could dance.

—MARIE BROOKS

To dance the polka, men and women must have hearts that beat high and strong.
Tell me how you do the polka, and I will tell you how you love.

—PERROT & ROBERT

In the dance, even the weakest can do wonders.
—KARL GROSS

Dancing is the loftiest, the most moving, the most beautiful of the arts, because it is no mere translation or abstraction from life; it is life itself.

—HAVELOCK ELLIS

A dance is a measured pace, as a verse is a measured speech.
—FRANCIS BACON

The real reason I dance is because I want to explode.

—BILL EVANS

Young dancers are like leaves—blow on them, and they move.
—SIR FREDERIC ASHTON

I see myself standing on a hill behind our old farmhouse in New Jersey, lifting my arms in an unconscious gesture of oneness towards the round silvery glory of the moon. At the same time, I'm listening to the whisper of a faint breeze as it gently sways the tips of the tall pines. I begin to move. It is my first dance urge to relate myself to the cosmic rhythm.

—RUTH ST. DENIS

A dancer rises into a different kind of time,
a time made visible by dancing.
                                   —JAMAKE HIGHWATER

I never said no to anything
that had to do with dancing.
—ANNABELLE GAMSON

Dance has existed since the beginning of time—as ritual, as recreation, as spectacle.

—NANCY REYNOLDS

Learning to walk set you free—learning to dance gives you the greatest freedom of all: to express with your whole self the person you are.

—MELISSA HAYDEN

Dance is an excellent amusement for young people, especially for those of sedentary occupations. Its excellence consists in exciting a cheerfulness of the mind, highly essential to health; in bracing the muscles of the body, and in producing copious perspiration.

—NOAH WEBSTER

Concentrating for one hour or more on the manipulation of one's limbs relieves and refreshes a mind that may be overengrossed in emotional problems.

—DAME MARGOT FONTEYN

I realized that there was no character—whether a sailor or a truck driver or a gangster—that couldn't be interpreted through dancing, if one found the correct choreographic language.

—GENE KELLY

Now for a simple recipe for the enjoyment of modern dancing. When entering the theater, it is well first of all to leave as much of the intellect as possible in the checkroom with the hat. Merely relax and let the muscles do the thinking.

—JOHN MARTIN

I see the dance being used as a means of communication
between soul and soul—to express what is too deep, too fine for words.

—RUTH ST. DENIS

Dance is not separate from the life it comes from.
—MARIE BROOKS

Dance is concerned with the single instant as it comes along.
—MERCE CUNNINGHAM

My heart lifted my feet, and I danced.

—NATHAN OF NEMIROV

Dancing teaches you a sense of accomplishment. The discipline of dance teaches you self-discipline. You know you can achieve what you set out to do, not just with dance, but with anything you choose.

—MELISSA HAYDEN

We have a different bodily structure than most humans. Our spirits, our souls,
our love reside totally in our bodies, in our toes and knees and hips and vertebrae
and necks and elbows and fingertips. Our faces are painted on. We draw black
lines for eyes, red circles for cheekbones and ovals for a mouth.

—TONI BENTLEY

He dances because he is neither a vegetable nor a rock but a moving organism, and in movement finds release and expression.

—JOSÉ LIMON

The dance is a poem of which each movement is a word.
—MATA HARI

Audiences can be moved out of themselves on occasion, lured into another world. They may be, for a fleeting moment, opened to new facets of what they take to be reality. In some miraculous fashion, they may be brought in touch with themselves.

—MAXINE GREENE

"Wait a bit," she cried, "So you can't dance? Not at all? Not even one step? And yet you talk of the trouble you've taken to live? You told a fib there, my boy, and you shouldn't do that at your age. How can you say that you've taken any trouble to live when you won't even dance?"

—HERMANN HESSE

Dancing happens, dancing is always in the present.
—PETER MARTINS

A good dancer simply takes the physical movements of sport, exaggerates them, extends them, and distorts them in order to show what he wants to say more clearly and more strongly.

—GENE KELLY

It is not enough to want to be a dancer in order to be able to become one. Here the body has the first and final word.

—EUGENE GILSON

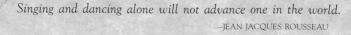

Singing and dancing alone will not advance one in the world.

—JEAN JACQUES ROUSSEAU

Dance is the only art in which we ourselves
are the stuff of which it is made.

—TED SHAWN

Graceful movement is just the right amount of energy for what you're doing.

—MICHAEL BALLARD

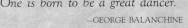

One is born to be a great dancer.
—GEORGE BALANCHINE

Mr. Balanchine is known to like those who fall; it indicates an energy and fearlessness that is essential to excitement.

—TONI BENTLEY

Nothing is more revealing than movement.

—MARTHA GRAHAM

Many other women have kicked higher, balanced longer, or turned faster. These are poor substitutes for passion.

—AGNES DE MILLE

A happy recollection from my early days at New York City Ballet is that feeling of anticipation at the beginning of each season when we would crack open those boxes packed with new tights.

—LISA DE RIBERE

He that lives in hope dances without music.
—GEORGE HERBERT

We dancers are able to transfer an experience to another. The body sends a message from a giving muscle to a receiving muscle; the spirit sends a current of emotion to a receiving emotion.

—PAULINE KONER

Dancing appears glamorous, easy, delightful. But the path to the paradise of that achievement is not easier than any other. There is fatigue so great that the body cries, even in its sleep. There are times of complete frustration; there are daily small deaths.

—MARTHA GRAHAM

When I was young, I danced all day and sometimes all night. But the dancer is like the boxer—he has to have the discipline of constant training.

—GENE KELLY

Fresh from her rehearsal and enchantingly full of herself, Betsy amused us by re-
counting the horrors of her self-sacrificing vocation—a cross, as she described it,
between the life of a boxer and the life of a nun.

—PHILIP ROTH

The dancer will never cut her rehearsals, but clamor for more, and when she is not dancing, she watches others, in acute discomfort, for she will make every movement inwardly and suffer with every fault.

—ARNOLD HASKELL

Woe to the dancer who loses patience! He will never find the way to the essence, to the resources and innermost motive of his dance. Never can he become a body of expression of all those things beyond his own ego, which reaches, embraces, and stirs other people.

—MARY WIGMAN

All those years I would feel after the ballet like a runner who had put his last ounce of effort into the race—the glorious satisfaction of having given everything to the moment.

—DAME MARGOT FONTEYN

To have a muscle warmed up and toned and ready to do something—it's a marvelous, sensual feeling. Then to feel and sense the quality of a movement, to have it inside, absolutely in the middle of your muscles, so that it can emanate and move and come out.

—EDWARD VILLELLA

In a dancer's body, we as audience must see ourselves—something of the miracle that is a human being, motivated, disciplined, concentrated.

—MARTHA GRAHAM

O body swayed to music, O brightening glance,
How can we know the dancer from the dance?

—WILLIAM BUTLER YEATS

The art of dancing stands at the source of all the arts that express themselves first in the human person.

—HAVELOCK ELLIS

Nothing so clearly and inevitably reveals the inner man than movement and gesture. It is quite possible, if one chooses, to conceal and dissimulate behind words or paintings or statues or other forms of human expression, but the moment you move you stand revealed, for good or ill, for what you are.

—DORIS HUMPHREY

Dance is, above all, a form of theater.
And like theater, it is unpredictable.

—NORMAN LLOYD

I do think people who come to see us get the feeling it could be themselves we're talking about—or dancing about—or it could be someone they know; and they get to understand themselves more.

—ANONYMOUS DANCER IN ALVIN AILEY DANCE THEATER

*Ballet is music first. My final attainment in dance is not step-perfect
choreography, but rather expressing music. My desire is to become the music,
literally, to climb into it, to explore it until I feel able to express it.*

—MARTINE VAN HAMEL

My well-filled curriculum—classes, homework, tennis, piano, editing—was ordered
with just one thought: to make room for the dance practice.

—AGNES DE MILLE

Slippery stages were the terror of my life.
—FRED ASTAIRE

Fred Astaire, when his miraculous feet are quiet, gives a curious impression of unemployment.

—HAROLD LOCKRIDGE

I took to wearing sandals because she did, even to parties, and when my
schoolmates teased, I scoffed at their fashionably distorted toes and said proudly,
"I have a use for my feet."

—AGNES DE MILLE

In a dancer there is a reverence for such forgotten things as the miracle of the small beautiful bones and their delicate strength.

—MARTHA GRAHAM

We love to dance that new one called the Civil War Twist. The Northern part of you stands still while the Southern part tries to secede.

—DICK GREGORY

It was a fresh, living experience for me at every performance as the drama unfolded. But when I left the stage door and sought my orientation among real people, I was in a wilderness of unpredictables in an unchoreographed world.

—DAME MARGOT FONTEYN

Most people feel they have to "fix" a dance, they have to make it "neat." No—it's better to have disordered life, but to have life. The modern dance is an individual quest for an individual expression of life.

—ANNA SOKOLOW

The value of the dance, its greatest value, is in the "intangibles." Success in the dance cannot be measured by a tape, weighed on scales, nor timed with a stop-watch. It demands an awareness and sensitivity in the dancer's soul and in the soul of the beholder who partakes, vicariously, empathetically, in the dance.

—TED SHAWN

*I think the reason dance has held such an ageless magic for the world is that it
has been the symbol of the performance of living.*

—MARTHA GRAHAM

Technique—bodily control—must be mastered only because the body must not stand in the way of the soul's expression.

—LA MÉRI

Dancing is a completely physical experience. You don't dance with your head, but with your body.

—MELISSA HAYDEN

I cannot remember a time when I did not love watching people dance.

—NOEL STREATFIELD

Sometimes dancing and music can describe a true image of the customs of a country better than words in a newspaper.

—GENE KELLY

Dancing is much like abstract painting: two viewers will be moved differently by the same dance, and the same viewer will be moved differently by the same dance seen on separate occasions.

—D. POHREN

Dancers work and live from the inside. They drive themselves constantly, producing a glow that lights not only themselves, but audience after audience. They
personify life itself.

—MURRAY LOUIS

It is not important that you should know what a dance means. It is only important that you should be stirred. If you can write the story of your dance, it is a literary thing, but it is not dancing.

—MARTHA GRAHAM

If you don't know what dance is about, it becomes just movement. It needs mean-
ing. Movement without meaning is just exercise.

—MARIE BROOKS

I dance far better for myself in front of a mirror. At least then
I know I have a receptive audience.

—TONI BENTLEY

A dance disappears as you see it. A movie of a dance is a dream. A description of a dance is just that. The nature of a dance includes impermanence.

—JUDITH DUNN

Throwing away a detestable leotard is an emotional experience unlike any other!

—TONI BENTLEY

A painting can be finished, but a dance can never be finished at rehearsal. Dance is a creation that needs the audience to be there, and only then can there be the whole creation.

—KEI TAKEI

She released us. She carried us through the rhythms and they were enough. The gestures were enough. There was no part of us pent up, unexpressed, to be taken home to ferment.

—AGNES DE MILLE